ONE STEP CLOSER

40 Doses of Motivation, Hacks, and Experiences
To Share with Millennial Catholics

Anthony Freeman, LC

ONE STEP CLOSER

40 Doses of Motivation, Hacks, and Experiences
To Share with Millennial Catholics

By Anthony Freeman, LC

www.branthonyfreeman.com

First Edition 2018

Copyright © 2018 Anthony Freeman, LC

ISBN-13: 978-1983441585

ISBN-10: 1983441589

Nihil Obstat: Jesús María Delgado Vizcaíno, LC

October 10, 2017

This book is dedicated to and asks the patronage of the unsung heroes, the non-canonized Saints who day in and day out glorify God, inspire us and make this world a better place.

They don't know who they are, but we do.

TABLE OF CONTENTS

FOREWORD

Success is the buzzword of our generation. We are constantly striving for success under the guise of "education" and "knowledge." But this success is one geared to money, fame, careers, and other avenues of worldly success.

This "success" comes at a price.

Mental health problems are on the rise. Family breakdowns are all too common. People are becoming more spiritual and less religious. Life for the average 20-something is hard, expensive, and stressful. Our economy is waiting to bust, our environment polluted, all whilst we ask the age-old question: "Who am I?"

In our work with Virtue Ministry, we've had our fair share of encounters with young people and their struggles in the modern world. Struggles from relationships, self-discovery, worth, as well as all the ethical dilemmas the world barrages amid that struggle of the human search for meaning. Amidst all the questions, somehow, a young person is meant to find that elusive work/life balance and be a modern-day saint. It can be a bit overwhelming, even daunting.

Who am I indeed, and who do I want to be?

For us, this is the real question. The answer to which negates all the confusion of the empty and shallow worldly success, and instead, draws us in a new direction; one where we become the best version of ourselves. The answer to which we've tried to help young people find for themselves.

In Br. Anthony Freeman, we recognized a kindred spirit, another person striving to help others grow in virtue and unleash their potential in a fresh and vibrant way. A necessity for a culture desperately in need of rescuing from the grip of vice.

He, too, encourages every person to recognize not only their potential but empowers them to become all that they are capable of, through the practice of virtue. *One Step Closer* is a brilliant way to start afresh, or to boost your perseverance. It makes the overall goal of holiness more achievable, attainable, and even enjoyable.

Br. Anthony's voice is real and tangible. His compassion and sincerity jump off the page and resonate loudly. He makes the striving in our spiritual lives, the speed bumps that pop up, and the humdrum of our daily lives meet in a balanced and manageable way. We all have such busy lives, but with short reflections and page-popping quotes, this book really does help you stay on the path of success, success beyond the worldly, in a way that doesn't feel like a burden.

He uses simple language that everyone can understand and gives you practical means to work out your strengths and desires. Br. Anthony also challenges you to be better, by showing you how to find areas in your life to improve, work through these habits, and set achievable goals. This book is like a modern, mini-handbook for being a Millennial Christian. It's a tool for ensuring that you are armed, prepared, and courageous enough to carve out your life and make a difference.

"Every person was placed on earth to change the course of history," Br. Anthony writes, and *One Step Closer* does that just that. It helps us change the course of our story, and consequently, of history.

Stina, Emily, Andrew & Matthew
Virtue Ministry Team

ACKNOWLEDGMENTS

My most heartfelt thanks goes to Angelica and Br. Samuel for, in ways unknown to you, you ignited the spark that made this book happen.

I would also like to thank Carlene Murray for her help with editing, but above all, whose support at the beginning was just what I needed to take this project seriously. I am also indebted for the selfless help and professional advice of Nathan Hadsall and Samantha Yee. Many thanks goes to Stina Constantine, founder of Virtue Ministry, for her helpful suggestions, as well as to Ryan Clear, Fr. Devin Roza, and Jim Fair.

Thank you to my spiritual director Fr. David Abad for never putting limits on the Holy Spirit or on me, and who could keep a straight face whenever I came up with another crazy idea!

Lastly, I want to thank my two families: my blood family, who has always given me unconditional support beyond anything that I deserve, and my religious brothers, who stand shoulder-to-shoulder with me and keep me grounded. To all who in great or small ways helped and supported me in this project, thank you!

IF YOU ARE HOLY,
YOU WILL CHANGE THE
WORLD

IF NOT,
THE WORLD WILL CHANGE
YOU

ABOUT THE AUTHOR

Hey! I am Br. Anthony Freeman, LC, a religious of the Legion of Christ studying in Rome for the priesthood. But you could gather that by looking at my driver's license (and also that I am a Louisiana/Texas hybrid).

I love mango gelato, swimming, and football, and even though I am a priest, I still enjoy listening to really loud music.

This is what's inside me:
- I believe God has created me from all eternity with a specific mission in mind.
- I love meeting and engaging people where they are at in their life.
- I want to inspire others through my personal testimony.
- I am passionate about helping others find their calling to leadership and evangelization.
- I rely on God's grace, value innovation, hard work, and generosity.

HERE'S MY STORY...

As a kid, I was adventurous, big-hearted, and entrepreneurial. I wanted to be a professional football player, or maybe a politician or businessman. No matter what I ended up doing, I had a firm conviction that I was going to do a lot of good in the world. I imagined myself traveling on my own, being independent, or even living in the wild for months at a time. I never would have guessed that I would be where I am today.

I grew up Catholic, but I wasn't very spiritual or even interested in the faith. I cannot tell you what my opinion of the priesthood was because it hadn't even crossed my mind as a possibility. Priests were guys that weren't able to convince a woman to marry them, I thought...

In junior high, all of the 'important stuff' (popularity, football, and girls) was going well for me. For some reason, though, I felt that my life was not heading in the right direction, mainly because of my group of friends at the time.

This wasn't a thought from the spiritual perspective; even in the worldly sense, I just had a feeling we were going to end up losers: addicted, narcissistic, dependent, in prison, or dead... an insight that proved to be true much sooner than I thought. I really didn't know where to go or what to do.

When I was fourteen and trying to juggle football practices and band camp one summer, I agreed to participate in a Catholic sports tournament in Baltimore. During the tournament, a priest gave a talk to the six thousand people that were there. But I felt like the only one in the room. He said something that struck me like nothing ever had before:

"You are only happy in life if you do what God wants of you, what God created you for."

Immediately, I felt very strongly that God wanted me to attend a Catholic boarding school for boys in New Hampshire and that I would be happy there. I still don't know why I wanted to go to this particular school, but I saw it as an adventure and a chance to find a new group of friends.

When I presented this to my parents, they were perplexed. In their minds, it had all happened so quickly and I had worked too hard in preparing to go to my high school to just change my mind. In a few days, however, they agreed to let me go.

Years later, my parents told me that this was the first time I had ever told them I wanted to do something because God wanted me to do it. Even though this was new and surprising to them, they had the faith to cooperate with what God had placed in my heart. They knew it was genuine because I wasn't smart enough to manipulate my parents by saying, "God wants me to do this..."

Even arriving at the school, I felt very at home. Through the most curious of circumstances, and by God's providence (or should I say, humor), I found out it was a high school seminary for young men discerning a call to the priesthood. At the time, I was not even open to considering the priesthood, yet since I felt at home, I decided to hang around. What this school gave me was a richer and deeper spiritual life that eventually enabled me to see that God might be calling me to serve him, and I began to see that as something beautiful and worthwhile!

Thus, upon completing high school, I joined the seminary, and God has gradually and beautifully revealed his plan for me. I have lived and worked in six different countries, studying, working at Catholic schools, and giving business ethics presentations or Vatican tours. Through it all, and after many years of discernment, I feel affirmed that God is calling me to the priesthood with the Legion of Christ.

Now, by reading this book, you are also part of my story...

INTRODUCTION

What began as scribbles of what inspired me has evolved into motivational videos on YouTube, quotes on Instagram, and finally, this book!

I hope to inspire and motivate you by sharing my personal experiences and insights and offering practical ways to develop and grow in your spiritual life.

The things that I share come from over eleven years in the seminary, discovering who I am and becoming a better person through the help of the Holy Spirit. My desire is to help you on your journey towards becoming the unique person God intends you to be!

I'm a firm believer in breaking large projects into small, achievable steps. This book consists of forty short messages that can easily be read and applied to your spiritual journey.

Sometimes I'll begin with deep spiritual reflections, then leave you hanging. This is done on purpose. I'm not trying to give you all the answers, but rather I want to provide a springboard for conversations you need to have with yourself, God, and others. Occasionally I'll also include questions for discussion and self-reflection at the end of the section.

May this book bless you on your walk towards Christ...

CONVERSION IS

A LIFELONG

PROCESS

#1 BEGIN THE JOURNEY, EMBRACE THE PROCESS

We hear Jesus say, "Be perfect as your heavenly Father is perfect" (Mt 5:48). But how can we ever reach God's perfection? As impossible as this call of Christ may seem, it teaches us two things:

1. It's about the process

Some people will hear Jesus encouraging us to be perfect and feel challenged and excited. For them, the sky is the limit! Others will hear this and fret. They fret because the only efforts they undertake are ones that promise comfort and rest at the end. They desire comfort and prefer to be unchanged and unmoved, whereas the call of Jesus says that this process of perfection will expand our horizons, exercise our virtue, and make us better people. Here's the thing, though. In this life, the journey of perfection does not end, and that is why so many people cop out. Their plans for greatness and adventure are too small. Conversion is a lifelong process, and this process is the greatest adventure we could ever embark on.

2. Our need for and the reality of God's grace

This mandate of Jesus also highlights that we cannot do this on our own. Only with God's grace can we truly have the ability to strive for perfection. It requires being open and willing to call on God's power to live his invitation to a life of holiness.

NEVER DOUBT IN DARKNESS

WHAT GOD HAS REVEALED TO YOU IN THE LIGHT

#2 HOLD ON TO GOD'S REVELATION

Every sunrise becomes a sunset, every summer is followed by winter, and every mountain peak climbed is also descended.

Few things last forever and most have a cycle.

Sometimes we have moments of extreme clarity in our lives in which we see things anew, like never before. There are times when God gives us a special grace and reveals a perspective, an attitude, or a part of his plan that we see with such clarity that we feel like we are above the clouds. We feel this way because we really have risen to new heights.

Most of the time, though, this clarity of vision fades and can even seem to disappear. We lose sight of things we once saw so clearly and believed so firmly.

There is a very valuable spiritual lesson here, though:

"Darkness does not equal doubt"

Just because you are going through a moment of darkness does not mean that you are doubting what you had once been convicted of. In fact, these moments of our darkness can enhance our spiritual senses to see things better than we ever did before. If, in these moments, you are able to hold on to what God has revealed to you in the light, you will be able to build on one conviction after another without the need to always start over. Never doubt in darkness what God has revealed to you in the light.

What is one spiritual truth that I once saw clearly but has now faded from its original clarity?

SOMETIMES SPIRITUAL PROBLEMS ARE ACTUALLY HUMAN ONES

#3 SOLUTIONS CAN EXIST IN OTHER PLACES

For years, when I would do my hour of prayer in the morning, I consistently fell asleep. It was quiet, I was in my room, the lights were dim, and prayer wasn't happening.

I thought that the reason I kept falling asleep and getting distracted was because my love for Jesus was lacking or that I wasn't trying hard enough. I gave myself a hard time, and as much as I tried to stay awake, I kept falling asleep.

Then, one day, I thought, maybe I couldn't stay awake because the lights were dim? Maybe it wasn't about not loving God fervently enough or not knowing the right prayer techniques. Maybe the solution was something as simple as turning on all of the lights, even if it meant a less comfortable and romantic setting. And it worked!

I learned then that challenges and difficulties in the spiritual life can have human solutions, and sometimes what we perceive as spiritual problems are really human ones.

Is it possible that you have some sort of apparent spiritual problem and are limiting yourself in where you are looking for the solution? Just because a solution seems "human" or "natural" does not mean it is not from God. Especially if your solution is motivated by a spiritual desire. God meets us in both divine and human ways. We are both body and soul; that is the beauty of how we were created and it is also the challenge. We are not purely material nor are we purely spiritual.

<u>Do I sometimes confuse human and spiritual problems?</u>
<u>Can I be more creative to find solutions for difficulties in my spiritual life?</u>

LOVE SO MUCH YOU FORGET ABOUT YOURSELF

#4 LOVE IS A GIFT

Do you remember the story of the poor widow who silently put two small coins into the Temple treasury as Jesus and his disciples watched (Mk 12:42)?

Look at what Jesus does not do...

- He doesn't reward this woman with a large sum of money.
- He doesn't tap her on the shoulder and say, "It was a social experiment. Here's your money back."

So what does Jesus do?

He leaves her gift at that: a gift, something that is freely given. But Jesus also focuses the attention of the apostles to see the love behind the widow's gift.

Jesus' lesson here is that giving a gift or doing something praiseworthy can oftentimes be motivated by recognition, advantage, or a kickback. Love is not motivated by these things, and that is the distinction that Jesus makes between her and the others. Love can put us in a position of being forgotten, humiliated, and exploited, which is exactly what happened to Jesus.

If we are going to follow Jesus Christ, the Son of God, who is Love, we must know that in this life we can and will suffer. We will have setbacks; we might even have struggles and needs like this poor widow. But we can also give our two small coins (which may even be everything we have) without expecting a reward or anything in return. And when we make this free gift of ourselves, let us not be surprised if God does not praise us or reward us, but rather let's be glad that he accepted our gift as a gift.

GOD GAVE YOU FREEDOM, SO YOU CAN RESPOND

#5 FREEDOM AND GRACE

Today there is a statue of St. Longinus in St. Peter's Basilica that makes up one of the four central columns around St. Peter's tomb. I have spent a lot of time in St. Peter's Basilica looking at this statue because Longinus' story perplexes me.

Longinus was a Roman soldier like all the rest. He probably drank a lot, visited prostitutes, and used bribery and extortion for some extra income. Just like the rest. The only thing that stood out about Longinus was a sickness in his eyes.

On an ordinary workday, Longinus confirmed the death of a criminal by piercing his side. He had done this to hundreds of previous criminals that were crucified. This was his particular job on the crucifixion team. This time, though, Longinus pierced the side of the crucified Christ, and as drops of blood fell on him, he suddenly could see clearly for the first time in his life.

Longinus was miraculously healed. He became a Christian, an evangelizer, and eventually a martyr for Christ. This brief contact with Christ on the cross changed his life forever.

Certainly, Longinus received a very special grace to have witnessed the crucifixion of Jesus, the earthquake at the moment of Jesus' death, and his own miraculous healing by the blood of Christ. Longinus did nothing to deserve this. What a grace! From then on, how easy it must have been for him to become a follower of Jesus, right?

Looking around St. Peter's Basilica, I can't help but ask myself, what about all the other Roman soldiers?

Didn't they also encounter Christ? What about the ones that scourged him or nailed his hands and feet? The blood of Christ touched them, too. What about the Roman soldiers that were posted to guard the tomb of Jesus and were the first witnesses of the Resurrection? Why didn't they become Christians? Why aren't they also saints? Why don't they also have a statue in St. Peter's? If it was so easy for Longinus, could it not have been just as easy for them, too?

The answer to this dilemma is simple: we are free to make our own choices. Like Longinus, the other Roman soldiers saw that there was something different about Jesus as they scourged him, mocked him, crowned him with thorns, and crucified him.

God's grace is present in our lives. The grace of conversion, the grace of sanctification, the grace of redemption is a free gift that God wants to give to every single person.

On that fateful day when the Roman soldiers saw Jesus, we can imagine that they were all offered the grace and opportunity of conversion, yet only one believed. St. Longinus' conversion was not a passive reception of Jesus' blood on his face. It was an act of free will to accept God's grace. The other soldiers also used their freedom. They freely decided that it would be too humiliating to follow this "criminal" even if he seemed to be the son of God. They freely decided that their current way of life was better than discovering this man on the cross and his message. They freely decided to let this opportunity of conversion pass them by.

Christ's blood was there for Longinus and for all the other Roman soldiers and spectators. God's grace is available to us today, both for those who aspire to be saints and for those who will turn their backs on God, and it is time for us to choose.

How will you use your freedom to respond to God's grace today?

GOD GAVE YOU FREEDOM TO LOVE

YOUR LIFE IS TOO BIG TO PLAY SMALL

#6 MONDAY PHENOMENON

In the seminary, we had Adoration on the first Friday of every month, where we stayed and prayed in front of the Blessed Sacrament through the night. I was sent to Ireland for my first two years of seminary formation and lived across from a business park with several buildings.

On one first Friday morning as I returned to my room around 4 am, I could see a few illuminated rooms in some of the business buildings. Most of the lights were on for the maintenance crews, but I could also see a few businessmen in their offices starting their day.

These people were getting papers organized, preparing contracts, and getting started on projects at 4 in the morning, and they most likely didn't have to be there at that time. During my time in seminary, the image kept coming back to me: the people in their offices who were killing themselves to make more money, get ahead, or get a promotion. Whatever it was for, it was clear that they were sacrificing their comfort and were focused on getting what they wanted.

The sight resonated a lot with me. It also bugged me a little, too.

Here I was dedicating my life to something that was eternal and transcendent:

- I was forming myself to be a priest of Jesus Christ.
- I was chosen by God and encouraged by others to be one who welcomes others into the faith by Baptism, sustains them with the Eucharist, heals them in Confession, blesses their commitment of Marriage, and prepares them to leave this world and encounter their God through Anointing.

29

This was my life calling, I thought, as I looked out the window onto the business park. Yet I constantly found myself dragging my feet, complaining about not sleeping enough or how inconvenient God's ways are at times.

The men and women I saw working in the tiny, brightly lit windows were motivated in their goals and they made the sacrifices necessary to reach them. After that moment, I challenged myself to embrace the dedication, sacrifice, and love that comes with my work and my vocation.

After all, what could be more motivating than doing the work that Christ has called me to do since in that I will find my fulfillment? Since then, the "Monday phenomenon" of giving in to tiredness and helplessness has not been a problem for me.

I realized then that my vocation is worth giving the best of me. My life is too big to play small. Instead of being exhausted because of the effort and sacrifice, I'm happier giving my all.

IF YOU LOVE WHAT YOU DO, MONDAYS WON'T BE A PROBLEM

START FRIENDSHIPS TODAY THAT WILL GET YOU TO HEAVEN

#7 FRIENDS FOR HEAVEN

Friendship is a huge aspect of our lives. We're more likely to trust a friend's opinion than an expert's, and friends can support and encourage us like a second family.

Just as we did not make the journey into this world alone, neither do we have to make the journey to eternity alone. I truly believe that after the Sacraments and spiritual help, good friendships are one of the best ways to help us get to Heaven and become the person God wants us to be. If you start to foster friendships worthy of Heaven, it will make it easier for you to get there.

"Show me who your friends are and I will show you your eternal destiny"

Our own personal goals and desires are mutually influenced by those of our friends. As a Catholic, my goal of getting to Heaven and becoming the best version of myself has to be accepted and appreciated by my friends because that should be what is at the center of my life and of who I am.

Your friends don't have to be holy to be your friends, but your eternal destiny and living in accordance with that destiny should never be drawn into question. Even as a seminarian, I have friends that are not necessarily strong believers, but they're all trying and they all support me in who I am and who I hope to be as a future priest.

We need friends for Heaven, but the first thing I can do is BE a friend that gets others to Heaven. My friends deserve the best of me. The consequences could be eternal.

Am I a friend that helps others get to Heaven?
Do I feel that my friends are helping me get to Heaven?

SOMETIMES LONELINESS IS THE

CONSEQUENCE OF BEING UNIQUE

#8 WHO I AM WHEN I'M ALONE

No matter how many friends I have or how close I am to my family, there is a part of me that will always be alone.

I'm not talking about experiencing a moment of loneliness. I'm talking about having a place deep inside of me that no one, no matter how much I reveal about myself, can truly enter.

After a while, I accepted that no one will fully be able to understand me.

At first this scared me, but then I realized that the place inside myself where I felt most alone was also the place where I was most unique, and it was in this uniqueness where I felt the most understood by God and the least by man.

Uniqueness can never be copied or fully understood. My gifts and talents and the way I look at the world is unique. This is God's gift to me and also our gift to the world.

Every human being is knowable and mysterious at the same time. I think a part of this mystery has to do with our uniqueness. So why not embrace it and find in it a special relation with God?

BELIEVE EVEN WHEN YOU HAVE OTHER OPTIONS

#9 GOD SHOULD NOT BE A LAST OPTION

Many people have found God and their purpose in life by hitting rock-bottom. When they arrived at a moment where they felt that they had no other options, they reached out to God and he was there.

But God shouldn't be a last option.

Happiness and spiritual growth consists in a correct ordering of our priorities and options, where God is not our last option, or even our second or third or fourth option, but our primary option. And you shouldn't have to hit rock-bottom to make this happen.

God as our primary option means:

- We share our joys and successes with him instead of only complaining about what is wrong.
- We consult him for guidance instead of only asking him to bail us out.
- We are confident in our time of need instead of being afraid.

Having God as a primary option implies having a relationship with him. A real relationship exists in all moments and not just in times of difficulties. Because God became man in the person of Jesus Christ, having a personal relationship with him is possible, and it is this relationship that gives us a sense of security that God will take care of us. God is always there. He is there before you hit rock-bottom, before everything is falling apart, before you desperately need his help, so believe even when you have other options.

Do I see my faith as a parachute only to catch me when I fall or as wings with which I can rise to be a better person?

37

I AM FREE
TO DETERMINE
MYSELF

#10 YOU HAVE SAID SO

At the Last Supper, when Jesus announces that one of his own disciples will betray him, they each go around asking Jesus, "Is it I?" (Mt 26:25). Unsurprisingly, Judas plays along and asks Jesus the same question, and Jesus responds in a peculiar way: "You have said so."

"You have said so" is the response Jesus gives to Judas, but he also could have said it to the other apostles that didn't betray him.

"You have said so" means "it is up to you."

We are free to do what we want with our lives. We write our own life script. We have more power over who we become and what our lives look like than we dare to realize. If today we asked Jesus as the apostles did during the Last Supper, "What kind of person will I be? Will I be a good mother or father? Will I make it to Heaven? Will I do good in the world? Will I fulfill my life purpose?", Jesus would give us the exact same answer.

"You have said so." That is, it is entirely up to you.

If we really want to get to Heaven, do good, or be an amazing spouse, then it is up to us to make that happen. It is up to us to work towards our goals.

We have the freedom to make our own choices. What we want out of life, and what we take the time to value and prioritize, is what we will get. Judas could have changed his mind about betraying Jesus. Even after the betrayal, he had the power to repent and seek forgiveness, but he didn't. Our fate is truly in our hands. God is not asking us to do it alone, but at the same time, your outcome is up to you. You are free to determine yourself.

ADMIRING A
VIRTUE
IS NOT ENOUGH

#11 UNHOLY HOLY THOUGHTS

Don't fool yourself by becoming content with holy thoughts. Just because you know a lot about your faith, admire the saints, or like the idea of living a virtuous life doesn't get you any closer to Jesus.

"True faith leads to action.
True prayer leads to change.
True admiration leads to imitation."

We can use holy thoughts, theological knowledge, and saintly stories to give ourselves a "spiritual high." However, when we do this out of a desire to make ourselves feel better, and not out of a genuine love and praise of God, it can stump our spiritual growth.

Just like we can trick our bodies into being less tired with caffeine, we can deceive our needs of spiritual improvement by thinking holy thoughts.

Empty holy thoughts can be used to inflate our ego. We feel a certain contentment because we think, "Hey, at least I'm attracted to holy things," versus others that openly shun holy things. This line of thinking is dangerous because it can lead to us becoming complacent and losing sight of the need to change and grow.

What did Jesus say about this? "Not those that say 'Lord, Lord' will enter into eternal life but he who does the will of my Father who is in heaven" (Mt 7:21).

Holy thoughts are good if they lead to holy actions. If not...be careful.

MAKE HOLINESS NORMAL

#12 AM I MADE OF DIFFERENT MATERIAL?

I think it's part of human nature to think that others, especially those that are successful, are made of a different material than we are. We look at movie stars, athletes, and other celebrities and tend to think that somehow they are fundamentally different from us.

The truth is, they aren't, and this truth also applies to the saints.

The saints were people that walked this earth just like us. They were not any better than we are nor were they any worse than we are.

If you keep thinking that saints are fundamentally different from you and their sanctity only depended on a special grace from God or the witnessing of a supernatural phenomenon, then I can almost guarantee you two things: you will never become a saint and your ability to improve your life will take much longer than it has to.

So what is it that sets a saint apart even though they aren't all that different from the rest of us?

The Church states very simply that a saint is someone who has <u>practiced heroic virtue</u> and <u>lived in fidelity to God's grace</u>.[1]

If you want to be a saint, then the task at hand will be difficult, but it is also something that you can start doing now with the very same material that you are made of now.

---

[1] Cf. Catechism of the Catholic Church #828

Here are some examples of how the saints were not made of any different material than we are:

- St. Jerome had a hot temper.

- St. Peter was very impulsive.

- St. Monica was married to an abusive alcoholic.

- St. Benedict Joseph Labre was mentally ill and a beggar.

- St. Drogo of Sebourg was really ugly.

- St. Rose of Lima was really pretty.

- St. Katharine Drexel was really rich.

- St. Bernadette was really poor.

- St. Calixtus was an embezzler.

- Bl. Angela of Foligno was vain.

- St. Olga murdered others in revenge.

What does "living in fidelity to God's grace" look like in my life?
Do I feel there is a particular heroic virtue God wants me to live?
Can I accept that God wants me to be a saint and admit it as a possibility?

BE HOLY

OR GO HOME

BEING HAPPY

IS THE GREATEST

TESTIMONY

ONE CAN GIVE

#13 IT'S NOT A ZERO SUM GAME

- Being holy is not about losing here on earth so that we can win in Heaven.
- Being holy is not only about the principle of delayed gratification.
- Being holy is not about suffering now so I can enjoy Heaven later.

Holiness in fact is not a zero sum game. We benefit, others benefit, and God is pleased. Some people think holiness is only about getting to Heaven or that the spiritual life is only about cashing in that eternal reward. This is only a half-truth.

We are supposed to be happy in this life, too. Holiness is part of God's plan for us both on this earth and in Heaven.

Following God's will, living a virtuous life, and being Christ to others all play a part in reaching our true potential and being happy here on earth. It's true that complete happiness is only possible in Heaven, but by being holy, we can begin to experience some of that heavenly happiness on earth.

This doesn't mean that we won't suffer or be sad, or that our lives will always be happy. The happiness of holiness goes beyond a fleeting emotion and becomes a state of being. Our human condition on this earth has its limitations.

A saint can and will suffer, but a saint is promised happiness. On the other hand, a heathen can and will suffer, but he will not be happy in this life or the next.

REMEMBER THAT SAINT THAT GAVE UP?

NEITHER DOES ANYONE ELSE

#14 LET'S BREAK IT DOWN

Talking about the spiritual life can seem very abstract. Getting to Heaven and achieving holiness can appear to be these huge, overwhelming endeavors. But what if we could break down the spiritual journey into smaller steps? What if we could look at the individual pieces of the spiritual life and see how they fit together? Maybe this could help us become more aware of how God may be working in our souls and enable us to better cooperate with him. At the very least, it would take away some of our anxiety.

Many saints and spiritual writers have done just this. They have analyzed and broken down the path for us. According to their observations, spiritual growth typically happens in three phases and can be experienced in a linear or cyclical cycle:

#1. Purgative Phase
- Someone in this phase usually lives in a state of grace[2] but may be attached to venial sin. This is the stage where we are purified of our worldly desires, attachments, and sin to be able to better hold on to God. You could call this the detox phase.

---

[2]As #2023 of the Catechism of the Catholic Church states: "Sanctifying grace is the gratuitous gift of his life that God makes to us; it is infused by the Holy Spirit into the soul to heal it of sin and to sanctify it."

#2. Illuminative Phase
- Now that the fogginess caused by our attachments to worldly things have been reduced, we can better focus on learning from and imitating Christ. In the illuminative phase, we develop and strengthen the exercise of Christian virtues and begin to see things that we couldn't in the purgative phase.

#3. Unitive Phase
- When a soul reaches the unitive phase, it is ready for a habitual and intimate union with God. This soul receives many spiritual consolations and can be happy even amidst hardship.

Everyone is different and the way that we develop spiritually can differ greatly; this is only a guideline of what generally happens. Usually a person who's just starting out on their spiritual journey will begin with a stage of purification. The process of detachment is not easy and can be accompanied by feelings of darkness. After all, it's difficult to let go of things that have given us a false sense of security or happiness.

It helps to map out these phases because it shows us that the first stage of purification is not all there is. Sadly, many never get past the first stage because they don't know how to suffer, which ultimately leaves them with a perpetual sense of dissatisfaction. Letting go of our attachments to sin and worldly desires hurts, but it allows us to fully embrace God. God's grace and love is so large and exclusive that we cannot hold sin in one hand and God in the other.

If you desire God but you're still in a stage of purification, I invite you to welcome the moments of detachment from yourself. With God's grace and your "yes," you will eventually move along on the path to holiness and come to know peace and happiness on a whole new level.

YOU DON'T NEED ANYONE'S PERMISSION TO BE HOLY

THE TERM CHRISTIAN SPECIFIES A TYPE OF RELATIONSHIP

#15 IT'S ABOUT A RELATIONSHIP

A lot of people tell me that they are spiritual but not religious. I applaud their spirituality, but I am confused that they deny their humanity. I am unaware of any human being that has achieved true fulfillment and happiness on their own.

Let me explain...

We humans are social beings. In families, on sports teams, and in school, we thrive when we get to share thoughts, emotions, and experiences with others and learn from others' examples. Likewise, our spiritual fulfillment cannot happen on our own; spirituality is personal but not private, and this social aspect is expressed in religion.

For our spiritual lives to thrive, we need help. First, we need the help of God and his grace. Secondly, we need the help of others. Just as someone becomes a mature, responsible person through trial and error, feedback from others, and role models, so too a Catholic can be spiritually helped through a faith community.

If we tried to get to Heaven on our own, it would be so hard. It helps to get feedback from our spouse, friends, and pastors, especially in the Sacrament of Reconciliation. It helps to have experiences of charity, forgiveness, and prayer with others. It helps to learn from spiritual role models, the saints, and members of our community.

What a blessing to have so many means to help us grow in our spiritual lives!

We do much better in community because we are social and need this interaction. We are fundamentally social beings because God created us for relationship with him. Becoming holy is above all about a relationship with God.

We see many different types of relationships throughout our lives. There's the relationship between teacher-student, parent-child, siblings, friends, coworkers, and the list goes on.

But what type of relationship do we have with God?

I would like to propose three that we can find in the Bible. We begin with a creator-creature relationship since we owe the entire universe and our very existence to God (Gn 1:27). Then Jesus reveals throughout his public life that we also have a father-child relation with God (Mt 7:9-11), and finally, at the Last Supper, Jesus calls us friends (Jn 15:14).

In the early Christian community and for us today, the Mass is a shared meal, and who do you have over for dinner? Your parents, family members, and friends. Sharing a meal is more about being present and being together than it is about being entertained. It's more about relationship than it is about duty.

The Mass is about the real presence of Jesus in the Eucharist; there could be no better reason to go. To participate in Mass is to be in His physical and personal presence, which is why Mass is not a "to do" but a "to be with."

Depending on our level of relationship with someone, we have corresponding greetings that reflect it. For those we do not know well, it is a handshake; for those that we are closer to, a hug or a kiss. Maybe the acts of genuflection, blessing, and communion in church are physical reflections of the relationship we have with God as creator (genuflection), father (blessing), and friend (communion/kiss)?

MASS IS NOT A TO DO

IT IS A TO BE WITH

PRAYER WORKS AS LONG AS YOU DO IT

#16 PRAYER

Jesus spent many nights in prayer. Sometimes he would even get up early in the morning to pray before the apostles woke. That's not normal, which means that prayer must have really meant something to Jesus. The apostles saw this and desired to pray the way Jesus prayed. They wanted what Jesus had; they admired what grounded him and his mission.

In my life, there are some things that I cannot let go of and prayer is one of them. I have prayed for a solid hour each morning for the past eleven years of my life. I also pray at moments throughout the day. Even after all the time I've spent in prayer, it's still a challenge and I still struggle, but I know that prayer works. I can't fully explain it nor do I fully understand it, but prayer works as long as you do it.

My experience is that prayer is not a goal to be achieved but rather a process, because it is the living dynamic between two beings, God and ourselves. The thing about processes is that they don't end. Praying is like learning a language: it takes immersion, it takes time, it takes effort, energy, and you learn to do it by doing it...

Even though at times it seems like nothing changes when I pray, I do notice the negative effects when I stop praying. When I stop praying the clarity of my decisions, the motivation of my actions and the joy of my life decreases.

The world is a spiritual desert and someone who doesn't pray will find their spiritual life dry up. We can only coast by for so long and coasting means settling for mediocrity. When we lose our connection with God because of a lack of prayer, the fulfilling of religious norms and practices become oxymoronic. So, pray and trust the process.

LET JESUS TAKE YOU OUT OF YOUR COMFORT ZONE

#17 GET OUT OF YOUR COMFORT ZONE

Do you remember the story of the blind man Jesus cures (Mk 8:23)? Jesus enters a village and a blind man is brought to him, and instead of curing the man on the spot, Jesus leads him out of the village.

But why does Jesus do this?

What is the village to this blind man? Being blind, he needs to feel his way around, and the clusters of village buildings let him know where he is. In addition, there are always people close by if he needs to call for help or ask for alms. The little security this man has in his life is due to his proximity to the village. If a blind man leaves the village, he could get lost, robbed, or injured. The village was this blind man's comfort zone, and by leading him out, Jesus takes even this away from him. How dare Jesus do this!

Now, imagine the apostles on the seashore mending their nets. Jesus tells them to drop their nets and follow him. Their nets and the lake are their comfort zone, their way of sustenance and security. And they left it behind to follow Jesus.

We all have our securities and comfort zones. For the blind man, the village minimized the effects of his disability. It was a way of coping with an unpleasant situation.

In order for real healing to take place, Jesus will dare to remove these things from us or ask us to freely leave them. It's scary but it's better than staying where we are, so let Jesus take you out of your comfort zone.

Do I have a comfort zone that is keeping me from growing as a person? Do I have a coping mechanism that will only work short-term and is not truly addressing the deeper issue of my life?

EVERY PERSON IS PLACED ON EARTH

TO CHANGE THE COURSE OF HISTORY

#18 GROWING INTO MY EXISTENCE

You did not decide to be born, but you can decide the path of your existence.

When I was a kid, I had great dreams of being a hero, of helping people and fixing things. I believe we all feel a desire like this at some point in our lives, a desire to make a difference in the world.

Eventually I forgot about this dream. I told myself humanity was not worth helping, there was no longer any Sleeping Beauty to save or big dreams to fulfill. I still thought the world could use some change, but I no longer had anything to do with it. The only world I cared about was my own, and even that felt incomplete and dissatisfying.

My thinking changed when I discovered that God had a plan for my life. I had a reason for my existence, even though I still didn't know exactly what the plan was. The moment I freely accepted God's will in my life was the moment I stopped wanting to be anyone else and the moment I started truly being myself. I discovered that my earlier dream of helping the world was rooted in God's dream for me to help the world. This is what gave meaning to my existence.

We are so small, and yet we are called to change the world. God has placed us here precisely so that we can change the world. We have the power to change the course of history. There are some things that only I can do and the best way to fulfill God's plan is to be who I was created to be.

EVERYONE WANTS TO GET TO HEAVEN

FEW ARE WILLING TO DO WHAT IT TAKES TO GET THERE

#19 THE UNIVERSAL CALL

We may be able to agree that everyone is destined for Heaven and God, in creating us, wants us all to be in Heaven with him. It's harder to see that the calling to Heaven comes with a calling to holiness.

You may think that holiness is only for nuns and priests, and that for you, holiness is out of your reach, but here's the deal...

When the Church uses the word "saint," she means:

#1. Communion of Saints (all who are now in Heaven)
#2. Canonized Saints (those the Church deems as models, who have lived lives of heroic virtue)

Did you get that? The Church considers everyone in Heaven a saint.

Now, being a saint means they are holy. If we are destined for heaven, then God is calling us to be holy. This is the "Universal Call to Holiness."

And when God calls you to something, he will give you all you need to do it.

Holiness is taking on the characteristics of God, who is all goodness, truth, and beauty, while simultaneously rejecting all that is not God, such as self-seeking, lies, and distortion. If we really think about it, all that is God naturally makes us happy, while all that is not God naturally causes us distress. So let's stop seeing holiness as something added on to our lives, and instead, let's see it as part of who we are as persons that are happy, fulfilled, and fulfilling our destiny to get to Heaven.

TURN YOUR VICES INTO SELF-KNOWLEDGE

SELF-KNOWLEDGE INTO VIGILANCE

AND VIGILANCE INTO VIRTUE

#20 FIVE STEPS TO REPLACE YOUR VICE WITH VIRTUE

Virtue makes it easier to be aware of what is good, to choose what is good, and to do what is good. If you want to do the right thing in life, you will want to have an arsenal of virtues to help you. Virtue is not an end in itself, but it is the way to do good and get to God.

Action Items:

- Step #1: Take a piece of paper, date it, and draw a line down the center.
- Step #2: List your vices on the left and your virtues on the right. Leave six lines in between each vice/virtue.

Right now, it doesn't matter if you have a lot more vices than virtues and it doesn't matter if you couldn't list a single virtue. What matters is how you are going to be better. What matters is how you are going to grow.

When we see what our vices and virtues are, we begin to have self-knowledge, which is the first step for us to be able to overcome our difficulties.

- Step #3: Below each vice and virtue, write three manifestations of them in your life. For now, I'm only focusing on what to do about your vices. There is also an outline of these steps in the back of the book.

For example, let's say you listed that you are proud. Now, write the ways that this pride comes out. It could look something like this:

- I am proud:
    o I judge people and their intentions a lot
    o I am very defensive and often justify myself
    o I am quick to speak and slow to listen

- Step #4: Next to or below each manifestation, write some of the most common circumstances (with whom, when, where, etc.) that this happens, like so:
    o I am very defensive and justify myself
        ▪ With my boyfriend
        ▪ When talking about the (insert favorite NFL team here)
        ▪ During work meetings

When we can recognize how our vices manifest themselves and when they commonly come up, we can begin to be vigilant.

- Step #5: List some ways you can change and become virtuous in each of these circumstances/manifestations. For example:
    o I am very defensive with my boyfriend
        ▪ 2 ways I will grow in virtue here:
            • I will make an effort to apologize when I feel the tendency to justify myself and have a humble attitude toward my limitations
            • I will make an effort to show gratitude for the critiques I receive, which also opens me up to seeing the truth and good that may be in them

Only then can we move on from vigilance towards virtue.

Forming virtue is not easy. The virtues are all interconnected though, and when we start working on one, we reap the benefits of many. Just like someone who gets fit and undergoes a body transformation, their fat doesn't become muscle, but rather muscle replaces the fat simultaneously. Similarly, our vice is not transformed into virtue, but rather our virtue is replacing our vice.

We must take note that eliminating vice and forming virtues is a lifetime project. It does not come fast. The simple fact of having these five steps will not be enough. You will need to sustain your efforts with prayer, the Sacraments, God's grace, brutal honesty, and perseverance.

In order to avoid discouragement, don't try to do everything at once. Even if you listed ten vices at the beginning, consider choosing just one to begin. Even then, you may still need to focus your work on one manifestation and one circumstance of one vice. The goal is to become more Christ-like through virtue, so it is better to have real change than a huge plan that is too overwhelming.

As you get into the habit of observing your moments of virtue and vice, you will gain better insights on how they are manifested and what you can do to become more Christ-like in these situations. None of us stay the exact same person, so periodically you may find it helpful to repeat these steps. Even if you don't completely eliminate a vice, you can minimize it, and in that process, grow in virtue. Most important of all, God will see your efforts.

GOD'S GRACE
+ HARD WORK =

ANYTHING IS
POSSIBLE

#21 THE FAILING POINT

In the gym lifting weights, we talk about bringing ourselves to the point of failure. It's that moment during your reps when you don't think you can give anymore. Your body begins to shake and you use all of your might to finish your reps. We call this moment the point of failure when your body tells you to stop but you keep going. This is the moment when muscle growth happens. Reaching the failing point makes us stronger.

It is interesting that struggle and difficulty make us stronger, and the result of being stronger makes things easier and more tolerable. This lesson can be applied to both weight training and to life.

- We distinguish an athlete by the ease with which they perform an action, not by how much they struggled or how many failures they experience before they succeed.
- Likewise, a holy person is one who commits acts of virtue with ease. The aspect of the struggle is not the point of weight lifting or the Christian life. The point is to be strong enough to more easily fulfill our purpose in life.

If we want to be strong in virtue, we cannot be afraid of the struggle. Some people only stay within the realm of what is comfortable.

"I am comfortable with helping my grandparents, but not my brothers and sisters."

"I am comfortable with forgiving a stranger, but not my spouse."

But that will not help us grow. So, how do we get to a point of failure, and thus a point of growth, in our lives of virtue?

#1. God's grace:

- God freely offers his grace to help us become better persons and grow in virtue. In fact, some virtues (like faith, hope, and love) cannot be obtained by our own effort and are pure gifts from God.
- God's grace also acts in hidden ways. Unexpected circumstances, persons, trials, and opportunities may cross our paths, and God and his plan can be behind these events without our knowing. He gives us an opportunity that we were not looking for. He gives us an opportunity to exercise virtue.

2. Practicing virtue to the point of growth:

- Virtue is a positive force. Exercising a virtue does not mean testing ourselves or placing ourselves in occasions of temptation or sin. It does, however, mean that we can bring ourselves to do more good and reach higher than we have before. Is there something that you held yourself back from doing in the past because you didn't think you could? Were you afraid, lazy or gave into discouragement? With God's grace, you can try to make that step towards virtue again.
    o Maybe you weren't able to forgive someone for humiliating you in the past, but a renewed commitment to try to forgive them, even if it's difficult, will help you grow as a person.

It also doesn't have to just be about the past. There may be habitual situations where you can exercise your virtue. For example:

o   You hate grocery shopping and become grumpy and negative while shopping. This makes you impatient and judgmental with everyone in the store. This can be a moment to proactively grow in virtue where you normally slip up.

Jesus was God and man. He possessed perfect virtue, so it's not like he had moments in which his virtue grew. However, knowing Jesus fell three times under the weight of the cross and got back up again shows us how he brought his body to the point of failure, to a point where he could not physically give anymore, and kept going.

Jesus' physical "point of failure" is a testament to his love and dedication to our salvation. Can we give Jesus that same testament in our growth of virtue?

THE STAIRWAY TO HEAVEN IS BUILT ON ROCK

#22 THE FOUNDATION OF CHANGE

In order to be a better person or have a personal relationship with Jesus, you will need to grow and growth implies change.

Some of the things you might want to think about changing are:

- Where you attend church, how much time you pray, and who you hang out with

While these suggested changes are valid questions to consider, changes of this type will often not last if something else is lacking. The root cause of our change may be at a deeper level than the actual change we are looking for.

I believe the model of the six neurological levels of change can shed light on where our first effort should be focused. The premise of this model is that a change of a higher level reflects the reality of a lower level. So many times when a change is not happening at a certain level, it is useful to see if there is an inhibiting reason at a lower level. Likewise, when a lower level experiences a change, the levels above it change in that direction almost naturally.

These six levels of change are:

#6. Environment (external to you but the easiest to change)
#5. Behavior (how you really act in situations)
#4. Capabilities (behaviors that depend on skills or virtues)
#3. Beliefs (affect our decision-making, view of the world, and values)
#2. Identity (who I am or what I perceive myself to be)
#1. Purpose (why God placed me here, where I fit in)

For example, consider one who behaves timidly (level 5), and instead of trying to force themselves to behave differently, they could look at their social skills (level 4). They may not actually be timid, but rather just lacking in social education. With this education, they may be better able to change their actual behavior. Their timidness of behavior and lack of social capability could also be due to a limiting belief (level 3), such as feeling that they don't have anything to share with others.

There are more external levels of change, but right now, I want to take a look at the deepest and most internal level, the level of our purpose.

#1. My purpose:
- Why did God place me here?
- What is my place in the universe?
- Where do I fit in?

It is extremely valuable to continue to ask ourselves these deep questions. They are foundational to living our lives with direction and intentionality, which affects our identity, behavior, and beliefs. If we don't have a life purpose or deny the possibility of having a purpose, then true fulfillment is impossible.

So how do I find my life purpose?

1. Ask questions.
2. Pray.
3. Look at facts.

In order to assist you on your quest of discovering your purpose here are some guiding points.

- Facts of my purpose (can apply to everyone)
  - ○ God created me out of love and for me to live in a relationship of love with him.
  - ○ I am called to be with God and others in Heaven for eternity.
  - ○ I am a human with the effects of original sin and there will be many times when I am more attracted to other things besides God.
  - ○ I am a creature that is limited.
  - ○ I am a son/daughter of God.
  - ○ I have God's presence and grace at every point in my life.

- Questions to find my purpose (can only apply to me)
  - ○ How am I unique?
  - ○ What types of people/things inspire me?
  - ○ Where do I find a sense of fulfillment in life? When do I feel happiest and most satisfied?
  - ○ How do I best connect with God? Is it through nature, friends, music, service, silence, etc.?
  - ○ What activities make me forget about myself?
  - ○ What causes do I connect with and really believe in?
  - ○ What mission could God have created me for?
  - ○ What do I feel the world needs?
  - ○ What do I repeatedly end up thinking about?

If you are striving to be better and find that your behavior isn't changing, try clarifying the purpose of your life.

BELIEF INFLUENCES YOUR MINDSET

WHICH INFLUENCES YOUR OUTCOMES

#23 YOUR MINDSET

Your mindset influences your thinking, which influences your actions, which influences your outcomes.

The people that achieve what they set out for in life have a certain mindset. The people that sit around and let their lives pass by also have a certain mindset. Championship athletes have a certain mindset, so-so athletes have another mindset. Great intellectuals have a certain mindset and the student that just tries to pass his exams has yet another one.

- What is the Christian mindset and where does it come from?

The Christian mindset comes from our beliefs. Our beliefs provide the script from which our mindset develops an attitude and way of being.

- If I believe that God is with me always, I will have a mindset that is less fearful.
- If I believe God's grace supports me in fulfilling his will, I have a mindset of confidence in spite of the many difficulties I may encounter and my own limitations.
- If I believe that God can make me happy, I have a mindset to follow him where he leads me.
- If I believe the cross unites me with Christ, I have a mindset that can bear pain.
- If I believe God can see everything, then I have a mindset that does not worry what others think about me.

Our Christian beliefs will influence our thinking, our actions, and yes, even our outcome in life.

When I read the Christian mindset beliefs above, did any stand out to me and why? Do I agree or disagree?

FEAR
DISAPPEARS IN
GOD'S
PRESENCE

#24 MAKING A LIFE CHOICE

God is not present in fear. Jesus never told us our lives were going to be easy. He never told us we were not going to suffer and he never told us we would always know exactly what to do, though Jesus did tell us to "be not afraid."

We cannot deny that fear is a factor in our lives. We fear loss, we fear change, we fear the unknown, we fear pain, we fear being wrong. Many times this fear limits our capacity for choosing to do what is truly good. Our life becomes a series of reactions instead of intentional actions.

When considering a life choice, and thus God's plan for us, fear should have has no place in our decision.

- If you are called to a church vocation: When you are professing your vows, you have to be able to look Jesus in the eye and know that you choose this state of life not because you don't have any other options, but because you believe he is calling you to this. No fear.

- If you are called to marriage: When you are professing your vows, you have to be able to look into your spouse's eyes and know that you choose him/her not because you are running away from religious life, but because you choose him/her as your companion to Heaven. No fear.

GOD DIDN'T BRING YOU INTO THE WORLD TO BE AVERAGE

#25 FOCUS ON YOUR GIFTS

The parable of the talents reveals something that is very insightful and unique about the way we judge ourselves. To win first place in a race we just have to finish a second before the others. To be famous we just have to have more followers. To be the richest we just need a larger amount of money than the rest.

The parable of the talents flips this perspective and says,

"You were given this- what have you done with it?"

When we are face-to-face with God in prayer, or on the judgment seat, comparison to others fades away. You might be the fastest, but what if you could run faster? You built three hospitals (that is amazing), but what if you could have built four?

God is no fool. He is not asking us to be first place in anything. We don't have to beat others to please him, we don't have to finish first, we don't even have to reach a certain status of holiness. God is asking us to accept the gifts we have been given. God is asking us to be the best version of ourselves.

Each of us has a unique mission and we have been gifted very specific talents for the life God has called us to lead. The moment we discover our calling is the moment we begin to become aware of what we are truly capable of. I can dream big for my life, but I know that no matter what I've dreamed of, God's dreams for me are bigger.

Don't be average; that's not what God brought you into the world for.

IF HOLINESS WAS EASY,

EVERYONE WOULD BE A SAINT

#26 IF I ONLY WITNESSED A MIRACLE...

Sometimes we think it would be easier to believe if we were one of the "lucky ones" who saw Jesus walk the earth or witnessed his miracles or tasted the bread and fish he multiplied.

"If that happened to me, then I would definitely be holy," we say.

But the reality is, it's just as hard. There were a great number of people that saw Jesus' divine power and still refused to believe. Why?

"Because they didn't want to," and therefore they "chose not to." Why? "Because it was more convenient for them if Jesus wasn't the Messiah."

Some of these people were the Pharisees that Jesus butted heads with at various times during his public life. Some others were the Roman tax collectors, soldiers, and diplomats that surely heard and even witnessed some of Jesus' miracles. There were also the ordinary Jews that ate the bread he multiplied.

The facts were there, but their attachments to their securities, pleasures, and pride warped their way of thinking and inhibited them from seeing the truth that was before their eyes. The Pharisees were supposedly awaiting the Messiah, but in effect, he wasn't welcome.

When we say it's hard to believe because we haven't witnessed anything supernatural, could we actually be saying that we prefer it that way because it's more convenient?

Would I be ready to live my life like one who has witnessed a miracle?

ACT AS IF

YOUR HEROES

ARE WATCHING

#27 YOUR HEROES

Do you have a spiritual hero? It could be anyone; a friend, a mentor, a saint, or someone else whose faith you admire. If you don't have a spiritual hero, then I can bet you don't know where you're going in your spiritual life.

This is because a hero is someone who has achieved what we want to achieve. They've attained something that we hold to be valuable. If you value sports, you will naturally have athletic heroes. If you value fame, your heroes will be celebrities, and the list goes on if you value money, adventure, or music.

- Who are your heroes and role models right now?
- Are any of them spiritual heroes?

Let me ask another question. Do you know what you want to achieve spiritually? Have you asked God what it is? Can you describe it? And if you can, then chances are, you will begin to admire someone as your spiritual hero.

Having a spiritual hero will do two things for you:

#1. They testify that this goal I have, this desire in my heart, is possible and has been accomplished in the midst of reality and not merely in a dream world.

#2. They embody in a real way through deeds and attitudes what is many times something abstract. They prove my desires are real.

So let's challenge ourselves to clarify what we want spiritually, and we will naturally be able to find a hero to accompany us along the way.

Who are my heroes?

OMISSION IS THE GREATEST SIN OF AN APOSTLE

#28 MY BIGGEST TEMPTATION

As I was progressing through seminary formation and discerning my vocation, I began to discover some of my deepest fears. The commitment and sacrifices of the lifestyle were actually not the hardest parts or the biggest temptations to leave.

My biggest temptation to leave was my fear of failure. Not the failure of having left the seminary but fear of future failure in my vocation, failing to be an example, failing in my ministry. I felt that my vocation was very lofty and noble and I didn't want to risk the possibility of messing that up and causing harm to others or the Church.

Reflecting on it, this is exactly what Satan would want. If he could not allure me away, then he was going to try to scare me away. Even in my commitment, this fear of failure is still present. This fear also makes me think:

"It might be better to not start a project because the time is not right or I won't do it well anyway."

If Satan could not scare me away, then he is going to try to get me to stall. Sadly, this stalling technique has worked and there were times I did nothing out of fear of failure.

Doing nothing would be the greatest failure of my life. Through this internal battle, I have come to the conclusion that any good I can do today is worth doing. Any person I can help today is worth helping. If I do good today, I have not failed. Yes, in the future, I might fail, but if I am in God's hands, I need not fear.

I don't know how long I will be here, so why not make the most of it now?

HOLINESS CANNOT BE PUT OFF UNTIL HEAVEN

#29 SPIRITUAL BLUEPRINT

"Which of you, desiring to build a tower, does not first sit down and count the cost, to see if you have enough for completion" (Luke 14:28)?

Here, Jesus is not giving construction advice. He wants his disciples to be aware of the cost of following him, so that when they commit to him, they are ready for everything that it requires.

In our worldly endeavors, we develop detailed plans and blueprints to ensure our desired outcome. But how do we ensure that we arrive at what God is calling us to do with our lives? How can we "sit down and count the cost" to be holier men and women each day?

A "Spiritual Blueprint" can help with this. The spiritual blueprint can be a guide for the soul. It can help you:

#1. Focus on your vocation and God's plan for your life.

#2. Come up with a workout plan to strengthen the virtues necessary to fulfill your vocation.

#3. Provide a support system to help you stay on course.

There is no single formula for a spiritual blueprint; it will be as unique as you are. But I want to give you some tips that you can implement to create your own spiritual blueprint.

- Your Vocation
    o Step #1: Write down what you know or believe God is asking of your life in the general sense, meaning your vocational state. If you are unsure if you are called to (marriage or religious life), focus on your current duty as a student, volunteer, employee, youth minister, etc.

89

- Step #2: Write down what you think God is asking of you in the day-to-day of your life right now. Are there any particular virtues and attitudes or behavioral changes that you believe he wants? This should flow from your vocational state from step #1.
  - For these two steps, it may be helpful to envision the type of person you want to be when you get to the judgment seat before God.
    - What is it that God wants to see in you?
    - What do you want your grandkids or friends to remember of you?
    - What spiritual values are reflected in this?

- Your Workout Plan
  - Step #3: Write down an opportunity and obstacle you have to obtaining the virtues, attitudes, or behaviors you listed in step #2.
  - Step #4: Create a plan to take advantage of this opportunity and to overcome this obstacle. You can use the same steps from the section on replacing your vice with virtue, which in abbreviated form, are:
    - #1. List their manifestations.
    - #2. List their circumstances.
    - #3. List concrete actions that you can do that respond positively to these circumstances and manifestations.
      - These actions should correspond to the vision God has for you and who you would like to be.

- Your Support System:
  - Step #5: Write down three people that are examples of what you are trying to achieve. It could be a saint, a friend, or even a celebrity. The idea is that they inspire you towards your goal.
  - Step #6: List the names of at least two people that will help and support you in your spiritual journey. They could be friends, mentors, your parents, spouse, spiritual director, priest, and/or someone that you can share your spiritual goals with and who will pray for you and hold you accountable.
  - Step #7: Once you have identified your support people, share with them the vision that you believe God is calling you to and ask them to help you towards that goal.

This spiritual blueprint is only a means to help you reach your full potential as a person. It can and should be flexible to the outpourings of God's grace and situations that arise in our lives. By having a vision, a plan, and a support group, I have no doubt we will draw closer to what God is asking of us.

In conclusion, it's important to note that achievement in the spiritual life is actually not about achieving anything in particular. It would be so much easier if our vocation were simply to build a hospital. Rather, the goal of the spiritual life is about the internal transformation of ourselves into who God has called us to be. It is that simple, but it is also that complicated and mysterious.

BE WILLING TO

FIGHT FOR

WHAT MATTERS

MOST

#30 SURVIVAL INSTINCT

Out in the wild you see the most basic instinct of creatures. It is the survival instinct. Regardless of the pain or challenge an animal encounters, it will do whatever it takes to survive.

Imagine how a fish fights back with all its might when caught, or how fast a gazelle will run to escape death by a predator. This survival instinct is the catalyst that moves animals thousands of miles for migration or forces them to adapt and even go for months without food.

As Catholics, there is one thing that we need to apply this survival instinct to, and that is living in a state of grace. We have to be willing to fight, to claw, to flee in order to stay in God's grace. There is no greater loss than the loss of the soul and there is no greater gain than the gain of grace. If our weakness does get the better of us and we sin badly, then we would want to immediately go to Confession to get back into a relation of friendship with God.

I am all about giving our all and striving to be the best and most virtuous version of ourselves. There is no room for minimalism for a Christian. Nevertheless, as a base, we have to have a conviction in our core that becomes an instinct of spiritual survival in which the state of grace is something we are not willing to give up.

Come hell or high water we will do what it takes to stay in the state of grace. If we have to adapt, so be it. If we have to make sacrifices, so be it. If we have to migrate or change friends or routines, so be it. Our relationship with God reflected in the state of grace is the most important aspect of our lives, both here and in eternity.

UNCONDITIONAL LOVE CANNOT BE DESCRIBED WITH WORDS

THEY WOULD ONLY LIMIT ITS MEANING

#31 PARTICIPATING IN A DIVINE ACT

In my studies at seminary, I have theorized a lot about true love and what it really is, but I found that I learned the most about love from meeting a brokenhearted mother who lost her only 28-year-old daughter.

"Love is Unconditional"

Unconditional is not descriptive of love. It is synonymous with love; it is love. If there is a condition, any condition, it is an attempt at love but not real love.

"Unconditional Love," or "True Love," is a divine act:

- This is the story of creation.
- This is the story of the cross.
- This is the story of salvation.

While real love may be a divine act, it can be shown to us through human beings. In fact, we most resemble God when we love unconditionally.

- This is the story of so many parents.
- This is the story of those that forgive those who hurt them.
- This is the story of truly loving God back.

THE SEARCH FOR

HAPPINESS

IS A SEARCH

FOR GOD

#32 OH HAPPINESS...

We are all seeking happiness. It is the one goal that I share with the seven billion other people on this planet. Wouldn't it be absurd, though, if someone was only looking for the minimal amount of happiness needed to survive or get by in life?

It is absurd, but I find that is exactly the way many of us go about in our search for happiness. Many people, Christians included, are minimalist happiness seekers.

A minimalist happiness seeker will typically ask the following question:

"Is this a sin?"

In other words, what is obligatory? What do I need to do so my conscience does not bother me, so I can continue my search for happiness in other places? These questions miss the point and ultimately are self-contradictory. Sin is morally hurting ourselves, becoming less of who we are, and that's why it hurts God so much.

The question that a happiness seeker asks is:

"Does this please God?"

Now, what is happiness? I am happy when I possess something good. The desire for happiness makes it natural for us to want what is good and avoid what is bad. Even when we mess up and make mistakes, we are really searching for something that is good (like sex and love), but end up buying into a false image of that good (like pornography and masturbation) that in the end hurts us (bad).

The highest happiness then occurs when we possess the most perfect and infinite good that exists, which is God himself. Which is also why we can never be completely satisfied with anything other than God. Heaven is attaining the best good, the good that all seven billion of us are ultimately seeking.

Being a minimalist in what we have to do so as to not sin is the same as being minimalist in our relationship with God, which means that we will receive minimal results in actually attaining our happiness.

This is the connection between morality and happiness. Morality is not meant to burden us, but rather it is meant to point us in the right direction toward God. Morality points us in the direction of true happiness and not the false image of happiness.

A Catholic, Christian, or one who is searching for truth is not someone that is fleeing from happiness; they are the ones on track to finding it.

When it comes to happiness, do not be a minimalist and stick to following the rules. Our relationship with God and possessing him as our one true good comes first before all rules. It is only from this relationship that these rules have any meaning, so do more than the obligatory.

<u>Is there something in my Christian life that I am treating with a minimalist mindset?</u>

GOODNESS IS ATTRACTIVE BUT IT ALSO OBLIGES

ONE LIFE

ONE GOAL

ONE CHANCE

NO QUITTING

#33 PERSEVERE

Most people can show up, but not everyone can show up day after day.

Jesus tells it the way it is: "If anyone would come after me, he must deny himself, take up his cross daily, and follow me" (Lk 9:23).

Jesus does not hide the fact that being with him implies a daily cross. We may not have trouble carrying our cross every now and then, but the challenge is to do it day after day. Perseverance does not mean we do not fall and it does not mean we are perfect; it means that we do not give up. Falling is not failing. Jesus fell under the weight of the cross. He had followers leave him and disciples betray him, but he never gave up.

Jesus was not a quitter, the saints were not quitters, and the apostles were not quitters.

- Did the apostles fall?   Yes.
- Did they deny Jesus?   Yes.
- Did they quit?   Only one and that was Judas.

Mother Teresa experienced darkness and desolation from God for more than forty years. St. Monica spent seventeen years praying and sacrificing for the conversion of her son Augustine. St. Benedict Labre tried multiple times to enter a monastery and was continually rejected. They didn't all immediately receive what they wanted but they all persevered, and today the Church calls all three of them Saints.

Being a saint and getting to Heaven may sometimes seem impossible for you, but if you persevere when you fall, you will get there.

YOU CAN'T CONNECT THE DOTS LOOKING FORWARD

YOU HAVE TO LOOK BACK

#34 CONSTANT ANALYSIS

Have you ever seen yourself work, walk, or talk? We do these things everyday, but we rarely observe ourselves doing them. Athletes, on the other hand, regularly watch tapes of themselves so they can be better than they were before.

In Christian spirituality, we have a tool that is like an athlete's tape review, and it's called a "Conscience Exam."

Usually when we hear about examining our conscience, we are remembering our sins in order to go to Confession.

This is one usage, but a conscience exam can be so much more.

- What if we could use the conscience exam as a way of learning more about ourselves and seeing patterns of behavior that are both positive and negative?
- What if we could learn to review the motions of our heart and soul as it experiences attitudes of envy, selfishness, generosity, and humility?
- What if we could begin to connect the dots of God's plan and action in our life? We could see where he has led us and possibly see where he is leading us.

Here are some simple steps to do this in a conscience exam...

Step #1: Find your location and time.
- The exam does not have to be long, but it has to be useful. You could do it driving to or from work, at your bedside, or in a special place of prayer. However you do it, finding a consistent location and time will be very beneficial in the long run.

- If it is hard for you to remember this before you form the habit, set an alarm on your phone. For example, set a reminder for the last 5 minutes of your lunch break.

Step #2: Get yourself in the mood.
- Find what helps you to focus on the exam. Put on background music or find silence, light a candle, or begin with a favorite or simple prayer like the Glory Be.

Step #3: Say an Act of Gratitude.
- Begin the exam by taking note of the things that you are grateful for from the past day or for the opportunities you have before you and thank the Lord for them.

Step #4: Ask, "What is on my heart and mind and why?"
- This is the central point of your exam. What has caused you peace and happiness and what has caused you frustration lately? Are there any patterns?
- Review the intentions behind your actions:
    o In which moments were you generous and patient?
    o In which moments were you selfish or judgmental?
- Review the reasons that made you react to certain events in a certain way:
    o Why were my feelings hurt?
    o Why did I do this act of service?

Step #5: Review your Spiritual Blueprint.
- By reviewing your spiritual and general life goals, you can compare your day-to-day with the big picture of God's calling for your life. This gives us an eternal perspective that helps us realize the futility

of many issues we can get hung up on. It can also help us find creative solutions to our situations.

- After a while, a regular conscience exam helps us connect the dots and see where God may be leading us, which we can then incorporate back into our spiritual blueprint.

Step #6: Pick one resolution.

- Our exam should help us find solutions to problems and not just state what those problems are. Once you have identified an issue, you need to see how you will avoid, prevent, fix, or confront the issue you have. For example, you recently lost your temper with your friend or spouse, so your resolution is to do something to make amends. It does not have to be complicated, but it has to be actionable, even if it's only to commit to saying a Hail Mary in the elevator.

Step #7: Offering and prayer

- Part of facing the future with courage is knowing that you have the strength to succeed. To tap into Christian strength at the end of your exam, you should offer to God your past, present, and future. This reminds you that your life is in his hands and that you have his grace.
- Lastly, conclude with a heart-to-heart prayer asking our Lord for his forgiveness in your failings and his guidance in your daily duties.

THY KINGDOM COME!

#35 OUR BATTLE CRY

One of the gifts that I have received from my religious community of the Legion of Christ is what I call my mission statement, or better yet, my battle cry. Jesus gave it to us in the Our Father. It is:

"Thy Kingdom Come!" (or "TKC!")

There are many opportunities for us to say this simple prayer.

- When you don't feel like praying-   'TKC!'
- When it is time to wake up-   'TKC!'
- When the world rejects you-   'TKC!'
- When Satan tempts you-   'TKC!'
- When your efforts seem useless-   'TKC!'
- When you encounter another obstacle-   'TKC!'
- When God challenges you-   'TKC!'
- When God blesses you-   'TKC!'
- When you don't know if you have the strength-   'TKC!'

We can put this battle cry on our lips, on our e-mails, on our status updates, on our homework, etc. In fact, these are the first three words I say when I wake up in the morning.

Everything we do can be offered to God. This is how we can make each day and each activity a prayer. It is one way to make holiness normal. These three words orient us toward our goal and help us focus not on ourselves but on God's plan.

CHRISTIANITY IS NOT A STATUS

IT'S A LIFESTYLE

#36 FIVE AREAS OF THE SPIRITUAL LIFE

If you need help figuring out the spiritual life, here are five key areas that you can use as a starting point to learn, reflect on, and analyze your own spiritual journey.

#1. Sacraments...the gateways to grace

The Sacraments are the gateways to grace and the pillars of our spiritual life. The recurring sacraments of Eucharist and Confession are indispensable for maintaining the spiritual strength we need for our lives.

- Do you feel that you know how to prepare for Confession well?
- What attitude do you have in receiving communion?
- Does the frequency with which you receive the Sacraments reflect your desire to grow in the spiritual life?

#2. Prayer...keeps the relationship flowing

We cannot constantly receive the Sacraments throughout the day. If the spiritual life is primarily about a relationship, then prayer is the necessary communication that allows this relationship to be nourished and grow in any circumstance.

- Does your prayer go beyond asking God for favors?
- Are you able to simply enjoy being in God's presence?
- Do you know different types of prayer and the best ways for you to enter into dialogue with our Lord?

#3. Discernment...helps us to decide according to God's will

Discernment in the Catholic context means to judge and decide according to God's will and plan for your life. The hardest thing in life is not just to choose between good and evil, but between what is good and what is best. Our lives are full of decisions; discernment helps us navigate this process and gives us greater peace and certainty that we are doing God's will even if at times we are mistaken.

- When you are making a decision, is God's will part of your criteria?
- Do you know what the steps of discernment are and how to verify your decisions for peace of soul?
- Are you flexible and open to changing your plans if that seems to be God's will?
- Do you understand that many decisions in life are part of a process?
- Do you have the patience to follow the process?

#4. Apostolate...our actions based in love

"The Love of Christ impels us." When we have a profound experience of Jesus, we cannot help but radiate the love we have received. The radiation of this love is expressed through apostolate, or mission. One way to see how I have allowed myself to be touched by Christ is to see how it translates to actions in my life.

- Do you have a desire for others to know Christ the way you do?
- Do you see the misery in the world due to a lack of Christ and want to do something about it?
- Do you take advantage of big and small opportunities to share Christ with others?

#5. Abandonment...giving God the space to act

As much as we try in our families, work, relationships, and even in the spiritual life, we cannot make true progress without God's grace. Because of this, we need to learn abandonment and trust that God's plan is better than our plan. Abandonment is not spiritual passivity. It is active, while at the same time, flexible in responding to the different motions of God's grace.

- Can you admit that you are not in control of your life? Do your acts show it?
- Does the thought of abandoning yourself to God's grace and plan scare you or give you peace?
- Do you trust that if you do your part and are flexible with God, he will take care of the rest?
- If God wanted to surprise you, would you let him?

A CHRISTIAN LOOKS AT THE WORLD DIFFERENTLY

#37 THE PARADOXES OF THE CHRISTIAN LIFE

Life is full of paradoxes, the Christian life even more so. In order to override our gut instincts, it helps to be aware of what these paradoxes are.

There are many things about God and ourselves that are a mystery. Yet, even though we cannot fully understand it, we see that it is true. Here are some paradoxes of the Christian life that I have experienced.

- What was once fear of God..is now awe
- What was once something to do....................is now someone to be with
- What used to be a sacrifice..is now an offering
- What was once loneliness..............................is now a calling to intimacy
- What we think God is asking............................ is really what he is giving
- What was once a restriction..............................is now a guiding principle
- What was once miserable suffering..................is now suffering with joy
- What was once losing one's life and self........................is now finding it
- What was once descending into service............................is now ascending into leadership
- What was once silence and boredom..........................is now prayer, conversation, and discovery

113

SUCCESS CAN ONLY BE MEASURED

BY ATTAINMENT OF HEAVEN

#38 SUCCESS

By simply looking at a bank account balance, you would not be able to distinguish between a businessman and one who has won the lottery. They both have a lot of money, but are they both successful?

Why does it seem that there is an unspoken law about success? This law states that before success, there has to be a great battle.

Success, when we look at it, always goes in one direction.

Up.

Success goes against gravity. That is why we will never fall into or stumble upon true success. I believe this is why there is always a great battle before one reaches success, because success is upward growth, growth is change, and change is hard.

This tells me something about success. Success happens when we are changed in the right direction. This change is part of a process that produces interior results that can stay with us for a very long time. You can lose something as fast as you stumble upon it. Sure, you can win the lottery, but if you have not changed in the process, you are still the same person.

There are many good things that we can stumble upon in life. Maybe you will stumble upon doing the right thing or thinking/believing the right way. However, you will never stumble upon virtue or good intention. This is because virtue is upward and never accidental.

The forging of virtue and piety changes us in the process. We are no longer the same person. Success in the eternal and full sense is getting to Heaven; the process of growing in our love of God and in the virtues as stepping stones to Heaven is what helps us get there.

If we want to be successful in the eternal and full sense, then we must be ready for the great battles ahead.

- To form virtue is upward ascent.
- To deny ourselves for the service of others is upward ascent.
- To bear life's burdens with humility and patience is upward ascent.
- To love others as you love yourself is upward ascent.

- Waiting until you are in a good mood to do something is staying the same.
- Only doing something religious when you have an ulterior motive is staying the same.
- Saying prayers or committing acts of charity for self-justification is staying the same. This is not upward ascent.

God reads the heart and he is aware of the battles we face that others may not. He doesn't look at your soul as if it was a checklist or bank account. God looks at your love; he looks at your effort of ascent to him.

We are all on different levels of the spiritual mountain, but God does not compare you to others. All he wants is for you to ascend closer to him.

God compares you to yourself. This is freeing, but also scary. God wants to see you change. If with God's grace, today you can be a little better than you were yesterday, that's all you need to make him happy.

That's success.

BECOME COMFORTABLE IN DISCOMFORT

THAT'S WHERE GROWTH HAPPENS

GETTING TO HEAVEN HAS NO PLAN B

#39 HOLINESS CANNOT BE PUT OFF UNTIL HEAVEN

If there's one thing that I'm certain of, it's that God did not place me on the face of the earth to not screw up. If that were the case, he would have been better off not creating me.

We can fool ourselves into thinking that the ticket to heaven consists in not having any major failures in life, but this view misses the "why" of God creating me.

I was created for a positive reason, for a purpose, for good. Thus, my mission in life is to fulfill that good. I may mess up along the way. I may have minor and major failures and setbacks, but no amount of failure changes the fact that I have a purpose for being here. Our ticket to heaven consists in holiness and our holiness is connected to God's particular plan for each one of us, which will be different from person to person. No personal failure will ever render God's plan for our lives obsolete.

When we die and stand before God, he will not ask us to recite Scripture verses by heart. He will ask us if we were who we were placed on this earth to be. Being holy is being wholly who God wants us to be. There is no way around this; there is no plan B. Our happiness is rooted in God's plan for our lives.

Getting to Heaven doesn't mean we were perfect in fulfilling God's plan for us, but his plan is our path to getting there.

NEVER STOP
DOING
THE GOOD

#40 IT IS WORTH IT

I will never forget this simple piece of advice that came as a personal note attached to the letter with my first missionary assignment:

"Never Stop Doing the Good"

This simple phrase has guided me and comforted me when confronted with my own limitations. The desires we have in life, our mission, and our circumstances can be very big and very complex. These lifetime projects can be broken down, and when we simplify it to the moment-by-moment, we realize it comes down to "doing the good" here and now.

I truly believe that good reproduces itself. No matter what I do, if I am doing some good, no matter how small, it is worth it. A small good done today encourages and produces larger goods for tomorrow. There are very few things in life that last forever. But the good that we do lasts forever.

I could have fulfilled my missionary assignment to a T, but if I stopped seeking and doing the good, in the end I would have accomplished nothing. Not to mention, focusing on doing good is a pretty good cure for boredom, selfishness, self-pity, and laziness.

So I implore you, whatever you do and wherever you are, never stop doing the good!

MAYBE YOU WON'T

BE A SAINT

BY THE END OF THE DAY

BUT YOU WILL BE

ONE STEP CLOSER

THE END

My Prayer For You...

I pray that after reading this book, you feel accompanied and encouraged in your quest for holiness. May a little spark be ignited in you that influences the person you are in this moment and the person you are constantly becoming.

May you see more clearly your call to holiness and truly believe that holiness is possible. May you realize that your happiness and sense of fulfillment in life is inextricably tied to virtuously living out the calling you have received, which is the purpose of your life.

By God's grace and Mary's example, may your convictions be stronger and your resolve thicker.

'For the Kingdom of Christ to the Glory of God'

Personal Journal Notes:

Worksheets and Questions for Reflection

Five Steps to Replace Your Vice with Virtue

Vice

- Manifestations:
    1. _____
    2. _____
    3. _____
- Circumstances:
    1. _____
    2. _____
    3. _____
- Ways to grow in virtue in this area:
    1. _____
    2. _____
    3. _____

Spiritual Blueprint

1. What do I think God is asking of me? In what general direction or vocation is God directing me to go with my life?

    _____

    _____

2. What do I think God is asking of me in my day-to-day life in my present circumstances? Are there any behavior changes God wants? Any habits or attitudes I can build on?

    _____

    _____

3. Write down one opportunity and one obstacle that you have to obtaining the virtue, attitude, or behavior that you listed in #2.
    a. Opportunity:_____
    b. Obstacle:_____

4. What concrete actions can I do to take advantage of this opportunity to grow and overcome this obstacle to my growth?
    a. Opportunity:
        i. _____
        ii. _____
        iii._____

b. Obstacle:

    i. _____

    ii. _____

    iii. _____

5. What are the names of three people who are examples of listening to God's plan for their life and whose stories I can learn from?

    a. _____

    b. _____

    c. _____

6. Who are two people who can support me on my spiritual journey? They could be friends, mentors, your parents, spouse, or someone else that you can share your spiritual goals with and who will pray for you and hold you accountable.

    a. _____

    b. _____

7. How will I share my Spiritual Blueprint with those listed above? (At a coffee shop, at church, over the phone...)

    a. Mentor #1:_____

    b. Mentor #2:_____

THE ANNUNCIATION WAS NOT

MARY'S FIRST YES

#41 BONUS HACK: MOTHER OF GOD

It would be impossible to finish this book without calling upon our Blessed Mother who is, by far, the greatest spiritual hack and example there is for our journey towards holiness.

Mary is the greatest testament of what God's grace can do in a soul. She had the most lofty vocation of being the mother of God, and yet she was completely human, just like us.

Mary teaches us that what counts is not the number of personal achievements or fame, but rather our fidelity to God. Very few of Mary's words are recorded in the Gospels, yet the impact of her words and her "yes" to God will last into eternity.

It is clear to me that the "yes" of the Annunciation was not Mary's first yes. Mary taught me that if we wait for something big to say yes to God, then he'll most likely never ask us to do something big. Holiness is definitely made up of a big "yes" or two to God, but it is just as true though that holiness is made up of many small, hidden, insignificant yeses.

Mary sustained both her big and small yeses through almost thirty years of a nothing-special domestic life with Jesus. She didn't get in the way when Jesus began his whirlwind of ministry and miracles, but when Jesus needed her most as he hung on the cross, she was there.

Mary fulfilled her life purpose in all of its simplicity and patience, pain and joy. So, if we need a hand getting to Jesus and giving our "yes," we can ask her. As she was always there for Jesus, certainly she will always be there for us, too.

Join my inner circle...

Want to be the first to get my reflections, thoughts, and experiences as they happen? Join my inner circle e-mail list.

Sign up at www.branthonyfreeman.com.

I Would Love Your Feedback!

This is my first big project, and being the perpetual learner that I am, I would really appreciate your feedback for future projects. You can contact me via e-mail at afreeman@legionaries.org.

Let's Stay in Touch!

If you want to follow along with my personal journey or receive "Catholic Life Coach" inspiration, you can find me at the following accounts.

Instagram: @catholic_life_coach or @br.anthonyfreeman

Facebook: Catholic Life Coach

YouTube: Br. Anthony Freeman

Website: www.branthonyfreeman.com

Praise for Br. Anthony Freeman's
'ONE STEP CLOSER'

"Millennials crave quick and insightful reasoning; this is the perfect book to give them a head start on their journey towards holiness."
Richy Orozco,
Founder of Catholic Connect

"You know you've got a good Catholic book in your hands when you slap the page and say, 'That's so true!' *One Step Closer* is book-slappin' good. Small nuggets of Truth and bite-sized gems from the Holy Spirit make holiness manageable in this book, especially for young people today. Though each step is described as little, like a baby step toward God, we found that some served to be giant leaps in our spiritual lives. And although simple and straightforward, there's nothing fluffy about *One Step Closer*. It's an answer to our challenge to 'walk the walk.'"
Caitie Beardmore & Michaela Glafke,
Nun & Nunner

"Br. Anthony Freeman is a gift to a world heading in the wrong direction. In his book *One Step Closer*, Br. Anthony has provided a practical roadmap for drawing us closer to God's purpose in our lives. To quote Br. Anthony, 'If you are holy, you will change the world. If not, the world will change you.' His book is a spiritual compass to guide Catholics of any age toward a lifetime journey filled with God's grace."
Richard Spoon,
Fortune 500 CEO & Author of 'Team Renaissance: The Art, Science and Politics of Great Teams'

"This book is like a modern, mini-handbook for being a Millennial Christian."
Stina Constantine,
Founder of Virtue Ministry

"*One Step Closer* is not just for Millennials but for everyone! In this step-by-step, easy-to-read, and easy-to-digest book, you will find daily motivations and exercises to take a journey to engage (or re-engage) in your faith at a deeper level. Each of the chapters could stand alone for a daily dose of inspiration and reflection to take the reader through a 40-day plan for growth and self-discovery in their Catholic faith, or it could be read cover to cover in one sitting. Perfect for Advent, Lent, or anytime you need a little extra motivation!"
Monica Rougeau,
Founder & President of Elevare, Intl.

"As someone who has worked with young adults for a long time, this simple but deep book caught my eye as one that answers many of the questions my guys and girls usually have: How can I know God? How must I live? What type of friends are good for my life? You can tell he knows by experience how to guide people in their journey through life."
Fr. Jorge Obregon, LC,
Youth Minister and Founder of Search Retreats

"Br. Anthony combines both motivation and new media to help Millennial Catholics aspire to holiness. A refreshing and much-needed ministry in the world today!"
Ryan Parsons,
Author of 'Young, Catholic, American'